Note for Parents

Crafts and activities are not intended for children under 5 years of age. As with all hands-on craft projects, the activities presented herein require proper adult supervision. Please note that some of the activities depicted in this book include the use of tools and supplies that if misused or used unattended may present a danger to young children. Prior to allowing a child to perform any of the activities in this book, please make sure activities are appropriate for the child's age level.

ISBN: 0-7172-8970-2

Published by Grolier Books, Danbury, CT.

Grolier Books is a division of Grolier Enterprises, Inc.

Produced by J. A. Ball Associates

Designed by Janet Pedersen

Production by Niemand Design

GROLIER
B O O K S

Disney's
Classic Holiday Tales with Pooh and Friends

A Timeless Christmas Treasury

By Jacqueline A. Ball
Art by Kim Raymond

Background Painting by Ruth Blair
Character Inking by John Brown
Activities by Lynn Brunelle
Activities Illustrated by Janet Pedersen

Contents

Pooh's Night Before Christmas

Based on "A Visit from St. Nicholas" by Clement C. Moore

'Twas the night before Christmas, and snug in his house,
Pooh stared out his window, as still as a mouse.
When what to his wondering eyes should grow bigger?
Bouncing over the snowdrifts, it had to be Tigger!

"I've been looking for Santa, but I couldn't find him!"
Tigger shouted as snow swirled around and behind him.
"And tiggers could freeze off their stripes in this weather!"
"Come in," Pooh invited. "We'll wait here together."

Tigger bounced 'round the rug and Pooh sat in his chair,
Both listening for sounds that meant Santa was there.
But they heard not a bell, nor the tap of a hoof.
They heard only wind blowing snow off the roof.

At last Tigger shouted, "I've got an idea-r-r!
Maybe Santa got lost and can't find his way here!
Let's make a few signs that the old guy can see—
So he'll know where to leave all the presents for me!
(Oops—for you, too, Pooh!)

"I think we should build him a honey-pot trail.
Then he'll find us for sure, yessirree, without fail!"
So they carried out pots and then came back for more—
There soon was a honey-pot path to Pooh's door!

Then Tigger kept bouncing across the deep snow,
Calling, "Hurry up, Pooh—we've got places to go!
We'll write a sign in the snow, so it's clear
That Santa can land here with all his reindeer."

So Pooh trudged up a hill, being sure not to fall.
His friend bounced ahead like a striped rubber ball.
(They didn't see somebody placing with care
Sweet Christmas treats for his silly old bear.)

At the top of the hill, Tigger bounced extra high
And then made a sign to be seen from the sky.
Then back home to wait went Tigger and Pooh,
Never seeing their good friends Kanga and Roo.

Roo bounced along just as Tigger had taught him,
'Til Kanga, his mama, reached up—*whee!*—and caught him.
They leaped through the snow and did not understand
They were trampling the place where the reindeer
    should land!

4

Oops! Tigger and Pooh had to come back for Pooh's hat
And saw Santa's sign was now trampled and flat!
"Hoo-hoo-HOO!" Tigger chortled. "Old White-Beard's
   been here!
These are definootly tracks of a sleigh and reindeer!"

They raced back to Pooh's, where the candy was found—
"You're right!" Pooh told Tigger. "He must be around!"
But they peeked up Pooh's chimney and gazed at his roof,
Finding no sign of Santa, no other proof.

"Oh, bother," Pooh sighed, "I just can't go to bed."
But soon dreams of honey pots danced in his head.
"Well, I'm waiting up," Tigger said with a yawn.
But then, like his friend, he slept well past the dawn.

So they never saw Santa, who finally came,
Bringing their gifts and then calling by name,
"Now Dasher! Now Dancer! Now Prancer and Vixen!
On Comet! On Cupid! On Donner and Blitzen!"
But they heard in their dreams as he drove out of sight,

"Happy Christmas to all, and to all a good night!"

Pooh's Christmas Stocking

"Why are the stockings hung by the fire with hair?" wondered Pooh.

"Silly old bear," said Christopher Robin. "The stockings are hung with care, not hair."

WHAT YOU DO:

1 Trace the stocking shape here onto a piece of paper.

2 Cut out the stocking shape carefully to make a pattern.

3 Trace the pattern onto both pieces of red felt. Cut the stocking shape out of both pieces of red felt.

You and a grown-up can make this fun and festive felt stocking and hang it up on Christmas Eve by the fire – with care, not hair!

WHAT YOU NEED:

- A grown-up (very important!)
- Pencil and tracing paper
- Two squares of red felt
- A pen that will write on fabric
- Squares of green, yellow, and blue felt

- Safety scissors
- Fabric glue
- Glitter
- A hole punch
- Paper clip

4 Glue the shapes together with fabric glue all the way around the edges, leaving an opening at the top.

5 Cut shapes like these from the other pieces of felt and glue them on your stocking.

6 Decorate your stocking with glitter by drawing lines with glue and sprinkling glitter on the lines. Let it dry.

7 Punch a hole in your stocking with the hole punch (you might need help from your grown-up) and thread a paper clip through the hole for a hanger.

8 Hang up your stocking!

9

Tigger's Striped Reindeer

"If I were Santa, I'd have striped reindeer," said Tigger, admiring his own stripes.

"Reindeer are grey," remarked Eeyore. "Grey. No stripes."

"But they must be striped underneath, Buddy Boy," hollered Tigger. "Or else they couldn't bounce, bounce, bounce so high and fly through the sky!"

Here's a stripy version of Santa's reindeer that you can make and then hang on the tree.

WHAT YOU NEED:

- A grown-up (very important!)
- Individually wrapped candy canes for the reindeer's body
- Pipe cleaners
- Little jiggly eyes (help your grown-up look for them at a crafts or sewing shop)
- Small red pom-poms
- Water-based glue

WHAT YOU DO:

1 Twist a pipe cleaner around the hook of a candy cane and make it into antlers as shown.

2 Glue on the eyes.

3 Glue on a red pom-pom nose.

You can make a whole herd to hang on the tree, or use them to trot across your packages as decorations. (Just don't eat them!)

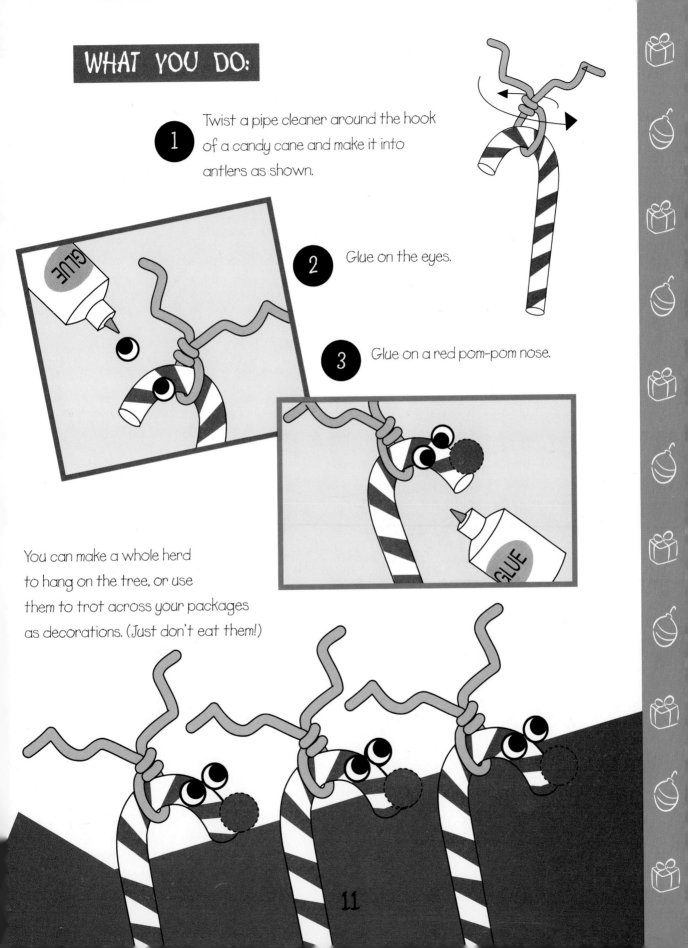

Rabbit's Christmas Carol

Based on "A Christmas Carol" by Charles Dickens

"Oh, can't you write faster, Owl?" Rabbit complained. "I need to know as soon as possible *exactly* how many carrots I have!"

Rabbit was making his yearly vegetable count. Owl was perched on a stool, writing down numbers in the dim light of one small candle. Every year, Rabbit worried that he would run out of vegetables during the winter. Every year he had plenty. But still Rabbit worried.

Owl peered down at his list. He cleared his throat. "You have abundant sufficiency, Rabbit," he said. "But dash it all, man! You should worry about increasing the luminosity in this structure. It is so dark that I can barely see my wings in front of my own beak. Why, it reminds me of that famous night when Great-great-granduncle Owl tried to relocate the entire northern flock. They had to detour through a cave at midnight—"

Rabbit groaned. "Owl, please! No family stories. We

have work to do. And there's nothing wrong with the light in this storeroom. Why use a brand-new candle when a stub will do? Waste not, want not!" Suddenly his floppy ears twitched. "What was that?"

"What?" Owl asked.

"That!" Rabbit exclaimed. "That . . . that . . . *crunch!*"

Rabbit poked his head around the shelves. "Pooh Bear!" he scolded. "You're supposed to be packing carrots, not eating them!"

Pooh was sitting on the floor, surrounded by heaps of carrots and boxes. Overturned next to him was a

honey pot. And in one sticky paw, Pooh held a half-eaten carrot.

Pooh looked up at Rabbit. "Oooh, I'm sorry," he said, "but my tummy felt a little rumbly, and I thought a small smackerel of something or other would help. And besides—"

Rabbit was already grabbing piles of carrots and stuffing them into boxes. "Forty-nine, three hundred and ten, ninety-five, oh, I'll never have enough! Besides *what*, Pooh?"

"Well, besides," Pooh said, "it must almost be time to stop working. It's Christmas Eve!"

Owl fluttered off his stool. He pulled out his pocket watch and held it up close to one eye. "Why, it most certainly is, Pooh Bear. It is now appropriate to consider a discontinuance of work." He puffed out his feathers and stared down his beak at Rabbit. "In other words, Rabbit, it's QUITTIN' TIME!"

Rabbit started to hop around the room. "Oh, no, oh, no, oh, no! We haven't finished! Christmas can wait!"

Pooh looked confused. "But if Christmas waited, it wouldn't be Christmas anymore. Would it, Owl?"

"That is quite correct, Pooh," Owl answered. "Christmas will *not* wait. Not for a bear, not for a rabbit, not even for an owl. We will gladly assist you another day, Rabbit. But I promised Kanga I would bring my special acorn stew to her Christmas dinner tomorrow. I must begin my preparations at precisely—" He peered at his watch again. "My word! At precisely half an hour ago!"

Rabbit pulled at his long ears. He pulled at his whiskers. "But Owl, please! You know I can't relax if there's work to be done. And there's *always* work to be done—for a rabbit."

Owl wrapped his scarf around his neck. "Rabbit," he said, "even *you* must make an exception for Christmas!"

Pooh wiped up the last bit of honey with a carrot stub. "Aren't you coming to Kanga's house tomorrow to celebrate?" he asked Rabbit.

"Christmas!" Rabbit exclaimed. "Stuff and nonsense! Bah, humbug!" He turned around and started counting carrots again. "Six hundred, twelve thousand, ninety-nine . . ."

"Come along, Pooh Bear," said Owl. "Let us make our exit while there is still enough light to find the door. It is clear that *some* of us have more *carrot* spirit than Christmas spirit."

Rabbit didn't hear them. He kept on working. He worked for hours by the flickering light of the candle. He packed boxes of carrots and bags of radishes. He neatly stacked pumpkins and cabbages. Only when the candle's flame sputtered out completely did he stop.

Rabbit sat down on the stool and wiped his forehead. He saw a few loose cabbage leaves lying around. "Waste not, want not," he thought. He twisted the leaves into a wreath. Then Rabbit closed the storeroom door and headed for his house.

"Who doesn't have any Christmas spirit?" he muttered, hanging the cabbage wreath on his door.

Inside his house, Rabbit felt very tired. "I'll make myself a nice cup of carrot tea," he thought. "Then I'll rest for just a few minutes."

Rabbit filled the kettle with water and put it on the stove. Then he sank down into his soft armchair. His whiskers drooped. His eyes began to close. . . .

Rap! Rap! RAP! Rabbit jumped out of his chair. Someone was knocking on the door. Rabbit flung it open and saw Owl standing there.

"Why, Owl," Rabbit exclaimed, "how nice! You came back to finish counting with me."

"No, Rabbit," Owl replied grimly. "That is not the purpose of this visitation."

Rabbit rubbed his eyes. Owl looked larger than usual. His voice had a strange echo. Everything, in fact, looked and sounded a little strange. "Well," Rabbit said to Owl, "why *did* you come back? I'm busy, as you know. I can't stand here all night."

"Why, my good fellow," Owl said, "I came to accompany you to Christmas dinner."

"Huh?" Rabbit turned his head toward the starry sky. "But it's still Christmas Eve. Christmas dinner isn't until tomorrow. You're much too early."

"Oh, no," Owl said mysteriously. "I beg to disagree. *Early* is most assuredly *not* the problem. My profound hope is that it is not too *late*."

Owl flew off, and Rabbit found himself following, tramping through the snow. Rabbit had no hat or scarf, yet he didn't feel the cold. Before he knew it, he was standing inside Kanga's warm house.

All of Rabbit's friends from the Hundred-Acre Wood were gathered, laughing and talking and singing Christmas carols. The smell of delicious things cooking came from the kitchen. Rabbit was suddenly very hungry.

"Owl, I—" Rabbit started to speak to his friend, but Owl wasn't standing next to him anymore. He was across the room, talking with Pooh. He didn't seem to hear Rabbit any longer—or see him. Neither did any of the others.

"Oh, dear," Kanga was saying. "Dinner is ready, and Rabbit still hasn't arrived."

Eeyore sighed. "Just like last year."

"And the year before," Christopher Robin said sadly.

"Doesn't Old Long Ears ever get tired of countin' his vegebibbles?" Tigger asked.

"Rabbit likes to work hard," Piglet tried to explain. "It's what makes him happy."

"But Piglet, it's Christmas," Pooh said. "Shouldn't being with his friends make Rabbit happy?"

"That's right, Pooh," Christopher Robin replied. "Christmas is a time to celebrate with everyone you love."

"Even *I* try to be happy on Christmas," Eeyore added. "After all, it's just one day. If I can stand it, so can anyone else."

"I wish Rabbit were here, Mama," little Roo said. "I put a carrot in his mug, just in case."

"Wait a minute!" Rabbit shouted. "I *am* here! Why can't any of you see me?"

There was no response. His friends couldn't see him or hear him.

"Merry Christmas, everyone," Christopher Robin said. "And merry Christmas to Rabbit, wherever he is."

"Merry Christmas, Rabbit," everyone said sadly.

Suddenly all Rabbit wanted to do was be with his friends. "I'm here! I'm here!" he cried out.

24

He hopped to the table and tried to sit in his chair.
But he fell right through it. He continued
to fall . . .

down . . .

down . . .

down . . .

He closed his eyes, and when he opened them, he was sitting on his own doorstep. Stars sparkled above him in the dark sky.

Why was it night again? Rabbit was puzzled but also relieved. Whatever had happened was very strange, but at least he was home again. Yes, he was looking at his tidy little house with its tidy front door, its tidy little doorknob, and the cabbage wreath—

"*AAAHH!*" Rabbit cried out. "It can't be!"

In the middle of the wreath was an orange-and-black-striped face. On the face was an enormous grin.

Rabbit gasped. "Tigger! Inside my wreath! Nooooooooooo!"

"Hey, Long Ears!" Tigger called out. "Howdee-doodee!"

Tigger's head popped forward. Then he sprang down from the wreath. He put his front paws on Rabbit's shoulders and bounced him all around.

"Tigger, please! Will you stop bouncing?" poor Rabbit pleaded.

"Nope," Tigger said. "No, sir-ree, sir. Not unless *you* promise to come to Kanga's house for Christmas dinner. You gotta be with your buddies on Christmas, Long Ears—not with your vegebibbles. That's what the old Christmas spirit is all about."

Rabbit thought of the warm, cheery group that he had seen laughing and talking and singing at Kanga's house. Then he thought of the mug with the carrot and of the empty chair—*his* chair. He wanted to be with his friends, celebrating Christmas, but . . .

"But, Tigger," he said, "Christmas dinner must be over by now. It's too late."

"Now, that is where you are wrong, wrong, wrong, Buddy Boy," Tigger said. "It's never too late for your friends! TTFN—Ta-Ta For Now! *Hoo-hoo-HOO! Hoo-hoo-HOO! Hoo-hoo-HOOOOOOOOOOOOOOO!*"

Tigger bounced off into the Hundred-Acre Wood.
His shouting echoed back to Rabbit's house. The sound
got higher . . . like a siren . . . a whistle . . . a . . .

"Teakettle!" Rabbit's eyes popped open. He was
sitting in his armchair inside his house. "Yes, the kettle
I put on for carrot tea!"

He jumped up and whisked the kettle off the stove.
Then he hopped to the front door and pulled it open.
The moon was just rising.

"Why, it's still evening!" Rabbit said. "I must have fallen asleep in my armchair. I must have dreamed that I was at Kanga's house. Then I dreamed Tigger was in my cabbage wreath." He shuddered. "Now, *that* was a nightmare!"

Rabbit's eyes lit up. "Wait a minute! If tonight is still Christmas Eve, tomorrow is Christmas Day. So it's *not* too late to be with everybody at Kanga's house. Oh, I hate to admit it—even if it was only a dream—but Tigger was right. It's never too late for your friends. But now I have so much to do. I'd better get busy."

Once again, Rabbit got to work. Once again, the hours flew by. This time, however, Rabbit was not counting carrots.

The next day, Pooh, Christopher Robin, Owl, Piglet, Tigger, Kanga, and Roo sat down to Christmas dinner at Kanga's house—just as they did every year.

"Is Rabbit coming, Mama?" Roo asked.

"Probably not, dear," Kanga answered. "He's probably busy working."

"No, I'm not!" Rabbit burst into the room. He dropped a big sack on the floor and rushed over to his friends.

"Yay!" shouted Roo. "Rabbit is here!" Everyone jumped up to greet their friend.

Christopher Robin pointed at the sack. "What's in there, Rabbit?"

"My special carrot pudding," Rabbit said proudly. "I worked all morning, making all sorts of goodies for my friends to enjoy. I have a pumpkin pie and a cabbage

cake, too. And that's not all. Look!"

Rabbit pointed out the window. Barrels of vegetables, each tied with a large red bow, stood in a neat row.

"There's plenty for everybody," he said. "What good is having a lot of anything if you don't share it? Merry Christmas, everyone!"

"Merry Christmas, Rabbit!" they all answered.

Piglet's Yum Pudding

"Where do candy canes come from?" Piglet asked. "Why, they grow in Santa's garden," answered Pooh proudly. "It's like Rabbit's garden, only it's full of sweet treats."

This candy-cane garden may look like dirt, but it tastes chocolaty-minty-delicious to Pooh, Piglet, and the whole gang! In fact, you could call it "Yum" pudding!

WHAT YOU NEED:

- A grown-up (very important!)
- 1 single-serving plastic container of prepared chocolate pudding
- Spoon
- Bowl
- 6 chocolate cookies
- Small clear plastic glass
- 4 small candy canes

WHAT YOU DO:

1 Use a spoon to empty the pudding container into a bowl.

2 Crumble 3 cookies into the pudding and mix it up.

3 Spoon the pudding mixture into the plastic glass.

4 Crumble the remaining 3 cookies and sprinkle them on top. Plant the candy canes and enjoy!

33

Rabbit's Garden Variety Writing Paper

"Look how handsome my radishes and cucumbers are!" said Rabbit proudly. "And my mushrooms and apples and pears. Why, it's a shame to eat up such beautiful things!"

WHAT YOU DO:

1 Have an adult cut the fruits and vegetables in half for you. These will be your stamps.

2 Paint the stamping side with a light layer of paint as shown. Press it down on your paper to make a print.

34

Fruits and vegetables aren't only good to eat. You can use them to make beautiful writing paper for notes to a certain big, white-bearded gentleman dressed in red (who has a habit of popping down fireplaces to leave presents for good girls, boys, and Pooh Bears).

WHAT YOU NEED:

- A grown-up (very important!)
- Assorted fruits and vegetables (apples, pears, etc.)
- Poster paints, nontoxic
- Paintbrushes
- Paper
- Colored pens or pencils

3 When your print dries, you can draw on it to make the prints into creatures or to create flowers or vines or a leafy border.

4 Write secret notes or send Christmas letters to friends—or Santa.

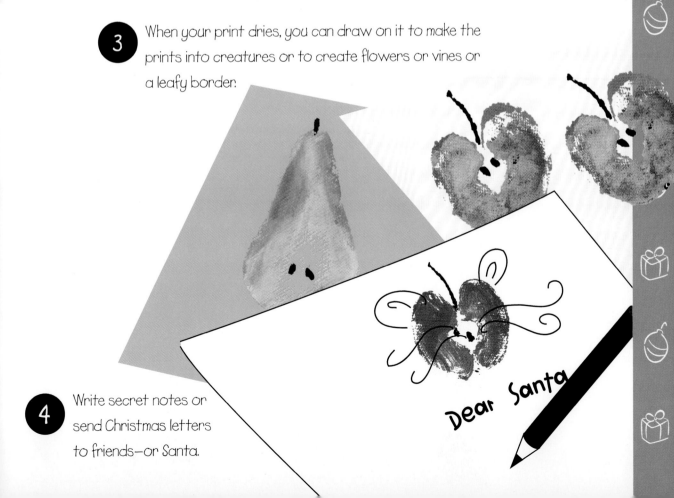

Dear Santa

The Twelve Days of Christmas in the Hundred-Acre Wood

Based on the song "The Twelve Days of Christmas"

On the first day of Christmas,
  my good friend gave to me
A tail ribbon on a fir tree.

On the second day of Christmas,
  my good friend gave to me
Two rare old books
And a tail ribbon on a
  fir tree.

On the third day of Christmas,
    my good friend gave to me
Three Pooh sticks
Two rare old books
And a tail ribbon on a
    fir tree.

On the fourth day of
    Christmas, my good
    friend gave to me
Four bouncy balls
Three Pooh sticks
Two rare old books
And a tail ribbon on a
    fir tree.

On the fifth day of Christmas,
  my good friend gave to me
Five honey pots
Four bouncy balls
Three Pooh sticks
Two rare old books
And a tail ribbon on a
  fir tree.

On the sixth day of Christmas,
  my good friend gave to me
Six pretty aprons
Five honey pots
Four bouncy balls
Three Pooh sticks
Two rare old books
And a tail ribbon on a
  fir tree.

On the seventh day of Christmas,
  my good friend gave to me
Seven red balloons
Six pretty aprons
Five honey pots
Four bouncy balls
Three Pooh sticks
Two rare old books
And a tail ribbon on a fir tree.

On the eighth day of Christmas,
   my good friend gave to me
Eight giant carrots
Seven red balloons
Six pretty aprons
Five honey pots
Four bouncy balls
Three Pooh sticks
Two rare old books
And a tail ribbon on a
   fir tree.

On the ninth day of
   Christmas, what a
   sight to see!
Nine snowy angels
Eight giant carrots
Seven red balloons
Six pretty aprons
Five honey pots
Four bouncy balls
Three Pooh sticks
Two rare old books
And a tail ribbon on a
   fir tree.

On the tenth day of Christmas,
   what a sight to see!
Ten chilly snow friends
Nine snowy angels
Eight giant carrots
Seven red balloons
Six pretty aprons
Five honey pots
Four bouncy balls
Three Pooh sticks
Two rare old books
And a tail ribbon
   on a fir tree.

On the eleventh day of Christmas,
    what a sight to see!
Eleven snowballs flying
Ten chilly snow friends
Nine snowy angels
Eight giant carrots
Seven red balloons
Six pretty aprons
Five honey pots
Four bouncy balls
Three Pooh sticks
Two rare old books
And a tail ribbon on a fir tree.

On the twelfth day of Christmas, what a sight to see!

44

Twelve Christmas stockings
Eleven snowballs flying
Ten chilly snow friends
Nine snowy angels
Eight giant carrots
Seven red balloons
Six pretty aprons
Five honey pots
Four bouncy balls
Three Pooh sticks
Two rare old books
And a tail ribbon on a fir tree!

Piglet's Paper Cup Angels

"I can make a snow angel," said Piglet. "But that won't last long on my tree!"

WHAT YOU DO:

1 Place your paper cup upside down on the white construction paper. Trace a circle. Then draw two long triangles. Cut out all the shapes.

2 Draw a face on the circle and tape to the cup as shown in the picture.

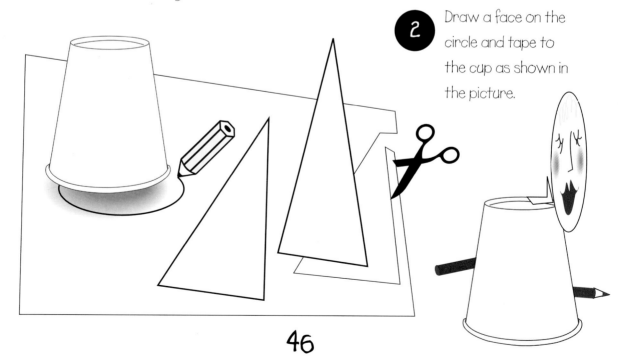

Here's an angel made of shapes that can perch atop your Christmas tree.

WHAT YOU NEED:

- A grown-up (very important!)
- A plain white paper cup (medium size)
- White construction paper
- Markers

- Safety scissors
- Tape
- Water-based glue
- Glitter

3 "Draw" patterns on the wings and cup with glue and sprinkle glitter over the wet glue.

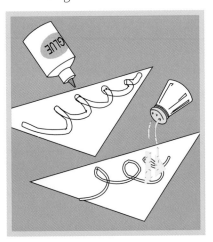

4 When the glue dries, gently tap off the loose glitter. Then tape the wings to the cup as shown.

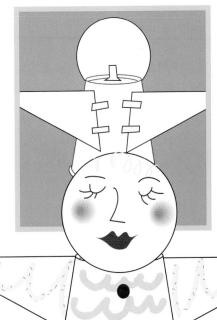

5 Use markers to finish decorating your angel.

Pooh's Christmas Jigsaw Puzzle Cards

"Oh, bother," said Pooh as he opened up an envelope and a number of puzzle pieces dropped out. "This Christmas card is all in pieces. How did that happen?"

"Do you think it broke?" worried Piglet.

"Of course not," said Christopher Robin as he gathered up the pieces. "It's a jigsaw puzzle. Let's put it together."

Send this puzzling Christmas wish to your friends.

WHAT YOU NEED:

- A grown-up (very important!)
- Old Christmas cards
- Safety scissors
- Piece of cardboard, 8 x 10 inches
- Water-based glue
- Pen

WHAT YOU DO:

1 Cut out pictures from old cards and arrange them in a collage on the cardboard. Try overlapping some of the pieces. When you are happy with your collage, glue the pieces to the cardboard.

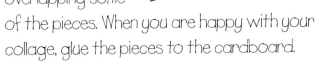

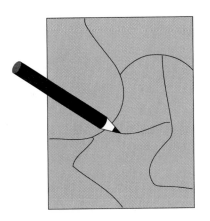

2 When the glue is dry, turn the whole thing over and draw puzzle pieces on the back with a pen. With an adult's help, cut these pieces out.

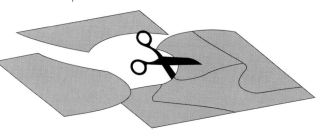

To Piglet
Pooh,
Hundred-Acre Wood

3 Now you have your own Christmas jigsaw puzzle card. Send the pieces — with a note from you — to a friend. Your friend can put the pieces together for some Christmas fun.

The Perfect Party

Based on "A Simple Bill of Fare"

Eeyore was resting in his little stick house when he heard a sound. It was one he had heard many times before, but it always made him shudder.

Boing! Boing! Boing!

"Oh, no!" Eeyore hid his head. "Why does it always happen whenever I get comfortable?"

Tigger came bouncing out of the woods. He bounced over to Eeyore's house, and stuck his head inside.

"Hey, wake up, Buddy Boy!" he cried. "Check out my new necklace! Do you like it?"

A string of holly leaves dangled from Tigger's neck.

"Can't say I do and can't say I don't," Eeyore replied. "Can say I'd like a little peace and quiet." He flopped around, trying to get comfortable again and hoping Tigger would go away.

"Aw, come on!" begged Tigger. "Tell me you like it. Puh-leeze? I got it special for Christmas."

"Special? Christmas?" said Eeyore. "It's just another day."

Just then, Christopher Robin and Pooh walked by, hand in paw. "Hello, Eeyore. Hello, Tigger. What's this about Christmas being just another day?"

"That's what it is, for the likes of me. Nobody noticing. Nobody paying attention. But I'm used to it," answered Eeyore.

"Hmm," said Christopher Robin. "That's terrible. We need to help you get into the Christmas spirit, Eeyore." He snapped his fingers. "I know! Why don't we have a Christmas party?"

"Wouldn't change anything," grumbled Eeyore. "Nobody would remember to invite me."

52

"Maybe you should give the party yourself, Eeyore," suggested Pooh. "That way you can invite yourself!"

"Don't know how to give a party," said Eeyore. "Never go to any."

"I'll help you, pal-o'-mine!" shouted Tigger. "Giving parties is what tiggers do best! That's why they call us party animals! We'll throw a wingding that's tiggerific!"

At that moment Kanga came by, with Roo skipping behind her. "What's tiggerific, Tigger, dear?" she asked.

Tigger blushed. He always blushed when Kanga called him "dear." "Eeyore and me are gonna give an extra-special, spectaculackular Christmas party," he told her.

"Oh, what a nice idea!" exclaimed Kanga.

"Hold on," said Eeyore. "My place can't exactly hold a crowd."

"You can have the party at our house," Kanga offered. "There's lots of room. In fact, you can go over right now and start preparing the refreshments."

Eeyore sat up so suddenly his head banged against his roof. "Refreshments? Who's gonna make them?"

Tigger put his front paws on Eeyore. "Relax, Buddy Boy," he said. "Tigger's a world-famous chef with the bestest, bounciest reci-pep-i-ties!"

Kanga smiled again and patted Eeyore's shoulder. "It will be fine, Eeyore, dear. You'll see. Besides, the only really important thing about a party is bringing friends together to laugh and have a good time. Now Roo and I will hop along and invite the others."

"I'll be bouncing you, Tigger!" cried Roo.

"I'll be bouncin' you, too, kid," replied Tigger. "TTFN! Ta-Ta For Now! Eeyore and I have got a whole bunch of work to do. This is one Christmas party folks will never forget!"

Eeyore groaned. "That's just what I'm afraid of!"

Soon Tigger and Eeyore were standing in Kanga's tidy kitchen.

"Might as well get started," Eeyore said.

Tigger bowed like a waiter in a fancy restaurant. "For everyone's dining pleasure, I will prepare Monsieur Tigger's famous Extra-Bouncy Fudge Surprise." He began bouncing around the kitchen, pulling pans and bowls and boxes off shelves and out of cupboards.

Eeyore covered his ears at the clatter. "Think I'll just stay out of your way," he muttered.

"First we take some flour. . . ." Tigger began dumping flour into a bowl, and a white cloud puffed up. Eeyore coughed and sneezed as flour got into his nose and mouth.

"Next a little sugar . . ." Tigger poured sugar out of a big bag, spilling half of it on the floor. Eeyore's hooves slipped and slid on the gritty stuff.

"Excuse me," said Eeyore through his coughing. "Don't you need to measure?"

"Measure?" exclaimed Tigger. He bounced onto Eeyore's chest and stared him in the eye. "MEASURE? Tiggers don't need to measure. Tiggers know exactically

how much of everything to use. Like this milk."

He grabbed a bottle of milk from the refrigerator and emptied the whole thing into the bowl. Some of it splashed onto Eeyore.

"Like I said, I think I'll stay out of your way," grumbled Eeyore, crawling under Kanga's kitchen table.

"Never fear, Buddy Boy," Tigger sang. He was shaking white powder into the bowl. "I've made Tigger's famous Extra-Bouncy Fudge Surprise millions of times. Billions! Gazillions! And this is Tigger's special ingredient—what makes it truly tiggerific—bouncing powder! I always carry some with me, just in case."

When the can was empty, he put one paw on his hip. "Something's missing. It's Christmas, so that means we need something . . . red." He grabbed a plastic bottle from a shelf. "Exactically right!"

Eeyore crawled out to see what Tigger was holding. "Hmm . . . ketchup," Eeyore said. "Never had any ketchup in my Fudge Surprise before. Then again, never had Fudge Surprise."

"That's because it's Extra-Bouncy Fudge Surprise, made specially for Christmas, of course! Everything Christmas-like has to be red. Or green." Tigger brightened. "Say, maybe we should add something green, too, like spinach or broccoli or some other vegebibble." He thought about that, then made a face. "Naw, let's leave it red. And now, partner, it's TIIIIIIIIME to mix things up!"

"Must be a wooden spoon around here somewhere," Eeyore offered.

Tigger sprang down on all fours. He stared right at Eeyore. "A SPOON? Tiggers don't need spoons! Fantastickal chefs like tiggers bounce their Fudge Surprise to mix it up! Watch me, Buddy Boy!"

Eeyore was beginning to feel more in the mood for hiding than watching.

Boing! Boing! Boing! Tigger sprang around the kitchen holding the bowl. Thick, goopy red stuff slopped out onto the messy floor.

"Wonder if I can un-invite myself to my own party," Eeyore said. He backed farther under the table and covered his eyes as the wild bouncing continued.

Boing! Boing! Boing! Boing! Boing!

Suddenly there was silence.

Eeyore crawled out. "Now what?"

Tigger pointed up at the ceiling. "I must have added too much bouncing powder," he answered. "My spectaculackular Fudge Surprise is stuck. It bounced right out of the bowl."

On the ceiling was a huge red mess. As Eeyore looked up, some of it dripped down on his head.

Tigger looked sad and ashamed. Eeyore felt sorry for his friend. "Too bad," he said. "But it was a good try."

From somewhere outside, they could hear voices laughing and talking. "Oh, no! They're coming!" cried Tigger. "What'll we do?"

"Try to clean up, I suppose," replied Eeyore.

Tigger bounced frantically around, trying to sweep and mop and wipe at the same time. Using his teeth, Eeyore squeezed soap out of a plastic bottle. "Turrr ah da wa-wer!" he mumbled to Tigger as he pointed to the sink with his hoof.

Tigger turned the water on as hard as he could. A sea of soapsuds billowed out of the sink and cascaded onto the floor.

"Turn off the water!" Eeyore yelled, just as the party guests entered the room.

Everyone stood there speechless, watching the two soapsuds-covered friends. Christopher Robin rushed over and turned off the water.

Then there was a great sucking sound above them.

"Oh, my!" cried Piglet.

The great mass of sticky red stuff unstuck from the ceiling and hit the floor with a great SPLAT!

Christopher Robin leaned over and sniffed. "It smells like . . . ketchup!"

"I know," said Tigger sadly. "You're thinking it would have been delicious, huh? Well, it would have. Yessirree,

it would have been fantastickal."

Christopher Robin patted him comfortingly. "I'm sure it would have, Tigger."

"What a mess!" exclaimed Rabbit.

"Don't worry," said Kanga. "If we all pitch in, we'll get the place clean."

"Sure we can!" agreed Roo.

"Yes, and anyone who thinks the party is over couldn't be more mistaken," Owl added. "We've brought the festivities with us!"

"Just in case things didn't—er, turn out exactly as you planned," Piglet explained. "Not that we thought you couldn't do a good job or anything. But we each brought something special from home."

The friends had brought honey cakes and pumpkin preserves, Christmas stars to hang up for decorations, Christmas bells to ring, games to play, and Christmas carols to sing.

"That's all swell and dandy," replied Tigger. "But I wanted to use my special reci-pep-i-ties."

Kanga patted him. "There's only one recipe for the best party, Tigger, dear, and it is this: equal parts of laughter, love, cheer, friendship, and thankfulness for being together."

"That's all anyone needs to make Christmas special," added Christopher Robin.

Kanga's Party Showpiece

Pooh sniffed at the bowl full of sweet-
smelling things in the middle of Kanga's table.
"This smells yummy," Pooh said. "Too bad
we can't eat it."

Here's how to make a delicious-smelling treat for
a nose-tickling display for your table.

WHAT YOU NEED:

- A grown-up (very important!)
- Oranges, lemons, and grapefruits
- A box of whole cloves (do NOT eat them)
- Ribbon
- Pen or pencil

WHAT YOU DO:

1 Choose a lemon, grapefruit, or orange and stick cloves into the skin of the fruit, pushing them in as far as they will go.

2 Put cloves all over the fruit. When you are done you should see very little of the fruit's skin.

3 Make several citrus/clove balls with different fruits and place them in a pretty Christmas bowl for a sweet-smelling display.

TO MAKE CLOSETS SMELL YUMMY:

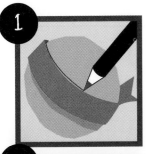

1 If you want to hang your citrus/clove balls, hold a ribbon around a fruit as if you were tying it around the middle. Ask a grown-up to help you draw lines at the ribbon's edges all the way around with a pen or pencil. This is where the ribbon will go, so don't put any cloves in this area.

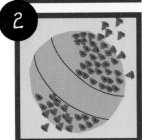

2 Stick cloves into the skin of the fruit, pushing them in as far as they will go. Put cloves everywhere except where the ribbon will go.

3 Tie your ribbon around the area where you drew the lines and make a knot. Tie another knot higher up in the ribbon so you can hang your clove ball.

Pooh's Musical Bees

"I just love bees," hummed Pooh as he walked with Christopher Robin through the Hundred-Acre Wood.

"But Pooh Bear! How about when they sting you and make you mad?" asked Christopher Robin.

"Oh, that's right. I meant I just love bees when they're making honey."

Make your own bees to play an old-fashioned game with a new twist. Don't get stung in this game of musical bees!

WHAT YOU NEED:

- A grown-up to supervise and make sure the game is played in a safe place (very important!)
- Black felt
- Yellow felt
- Glue stick
- Black marker
- Audio cassette player, radio, piano—any source of music
- Some friends to play with you
- Safety scissors

1

Take pieces of black felt and spread them out.

2 With a grown-up, cut a piece of yellow felt into three equal smaller pieces as shown. Cut each of those pieces into three equal smaller pieces. Glue three yellow stripes across each black piece with a glue stick as shown.

3 With a grown-up, cut each striped piece into a large oval. Now you have the bodies of bees!

4 Decorate your bees, using yellow felt and a marker to give them eyes. Make one fewer bee than the number of players you have. So if you have five people, make four bees. If you have six people, make five bees. (A grown-up can help you work it out.) Place each bee on a chair. A grown-up can be in charge of turning the music on and off. While the music plays, you and your friends go from bee to bee. Walk around the chairs. Make some buzzing noises. When the music is turned off, everyone quickly sits down on a bee. The player who doesn't get a bee is out! One bee and chair are removed, and the music is turned on and off again until only one player – and one bee – is left. That's the winner!

And to All a Warm Night

Based on parts of the Christmas carols "Good King Wenceslas"
and "We Three Kings"

Christopher Robin lay snuggled in his nice, warm bed in his nice, warm room. Outside the window, branches shook and shivered in the whipping wind. It was the first really cold night of the winter.

"I'm so lucky to be in here, nice and warm," he thought. "It would be terribly unlucky to be caught outdoors in the cold tonight."

Christopher Robin scrunched up his pillow under his head and stared at the ceiling, thinking about Pooh Bear. His chubby little friend had come to his door earlier to "borrow" some honey.

"Silly old bear," he thought fondly. He had given Pooh the honey and told him to take a bundle of firewood from the front yard.

The day had been so cold that Christopher Robin wanted to make sure Pooh had enough wood for a warm fire. "I'm glad to know Pooh is warm tonight, just like me," he thought happily.

Then a thought crossed his mind. He jumped out of
bed and went to the window. Sitting in a shadowy
corner of the yard was the bundle of sticks for Pooh.
His friend must have forgotten to take it!

"Oh, no!" Christopher Robin exclaimed. "Pooh's fire
may go out, and he'll get cold. I'll bring him the firewood."

He put on all the warm clothes he could find: socks,
boots, jacket, mittens, hat. Then he headed out into
the cold to bring the firewood to Pooh.

Meanwhile, at that very same house in which Pooh
Bear happened to live, Pooh was lying awake in bed.
He couldn't help noticing that the wind was howling in
that not very nice way the wind had of howling when it
knows it's going to keep on howling all night.

Pooh was warm and snug. He had forgotten the
firewood at Christopher Robin's, but he still had plenty
at home. So a warm fire glowed across the room as he
lay under an enormous pile of blankets.

Sighing happily, Pooh turned over, pulling the top
blanket up to his chin. The blanket was such a happy
color—a bright, cheerful red and pink.

Wait a minute. He didn't own a red-and-pink

71

blanket! Where had this one come from?

Pooh thought and thought. Then he had it. "It's Piglet's blanket! From when we had a tea-and-honey party on the grass. But it was summertime then, and it was warm outside. He might need it now."

Pooh heard the wind whistling. He couldn't bear the thought that Piglet might be cold without his blanket. Sighing, Pooh climbed out of his comfortable bed. He put on a scarf and mittens and went out into the woods, dragging the red-and-pink blanket behind him.

Meanwhile, in his little house, Piglet was awake, too.

He wasn't a bit cold, because his tiny body was covered with all the blankets, quilts, and warm things he could find. Earmuffs and long socks. Stocking caps and sweaters. There was a nice long sweater on top, with a big T on it.

Wait a minute! That wasn't his sweater. But whose was it?

After Piglet thought a minute, he exclaimed, "It's Tigger's! Now I remember. He got too warm from bouncing in the autumn leaves Pooh and I were raking. But tonight he might get cold without it."

So Piglet climbed out of bed and went out into the night, carrying Tigger's sweater.

Meanwhile, Tigger was perfectly comfortable, but he was worried about Eeyore. "That little shack he calls a house is mighty drafty," Tigger thought. "I think I'll bounce him over an extra blanket."

Eeyore was perfectly comfortable, too, but he was worried about little Roo, who had left behind a woolly stocking cap when they were playing Pin the Cap on the Donkey. Now he thought Roo might need it to keep warm. "I'd better take it over, just in case," he thought.

Little Roo was fine, but his mama, Kanga, was worried about Rabbit. She was afraid Rabbit might have fallen asleep working in his chilly storeroom. She packed some firewood into a quilt and popped Roo, wrapped in blankets, into her pouch.

Meanwhile, Rabbit was worried about Owl, because he hadn't seen him flying overhead the way he did every night. So Rabbit went to Owl's house to check. And because it was so cold, he thought he might as well bring along an extra quilt.

Actually, Owl had already flown by. But this particular night was so dark that Rabbit hadn't seen him. In fact, this particular night was so dark Owl couldn't see where he was going himself. There were no stars or moon to help guide him. Without realizing it, Owl flew far beyond the place where he usually turned around.

And so everyone was wandering, or flying, around the Hundred-Acre Wood on that VERY cold, VERY dark night. And that is why when friends came by with blankets and quilts and sweaters and firewood, they found no one home.

Christopher Robin was glad to find Pooh's house warm from the fire. But where was his Pooh? "I'll try Piglet's," he thought.

At Piglet's house, Pooh had already given up and was

74

heading for Tigger's. Piglet,
finding no one home at
Tigger's, went to Eeyore's.
Eeyore tried Kanga and
Roo's and then went on to
look at Rabbit's house.
Rabbit, of course, hadn't
found Owl at home and was
searching the skies for him. Owl
kept flying, farther

and farther away.

The deep, deep snow
made walking very
difficult, especially for
little Piglet. His steps
didn't even break
through the hard, icy
crust, so he kept going
around in circles without even
making a trail.

Poor Piglet was soon totally
lost as well as very tired
and cold.

Then something

amazing happened. A huge star came out and lit up the whole sky. The shadowy, snow-covered ground suddenly turned a bright, gleaming white.

Now Piglet could see tracks. And wait! Those weren't just any old tracks! They were hop marks! "Kanga must be right ahead of me!" he thought happily.

With a cheer, Piglet leaped inside the tracks Kanga had left. He followed them through the brightening night, thinking how much easier walking in deep snow was when a bigger friend left a trail for you.

By now the whole Hundred-Acre Wood seemed to be glimmering in the glow of the enormous star. Now everyone could spot someone else's tracks. They all used the trails their friends had made in the snow to make their own walking easier.

The friends walked faster and faster and soon . . .

Somehow they all ended up outside Eeyore's house at exactly the same time! They collapsed in a huge pile of laughter and blankets and sweaters. But after they caught their breath and realized what had happened, they noticed someone was missing.

"Where's Owl?" asked Christopher Robin.

"Let my presence be duly recorded," said a familiar voice as Owl swooped down. "But dash it all, it was dark up there! Without that star, why, I might never have found my way back."

The wind was becoming calmer, and the night no longer seemed so cold. A huge silver moon came out and joined the star to light up the Hundred-Acre Wood even more. Thousands of other stars came out and began to twinkle and gleam. The night grew calm and peaceful.

And in that calm, peaceful night, Christopher Robin
and his friends went to Pooh's house and crowded
together under all their warm things. And, one by one,
they fell fast asleep.

Hundred-Acre Wood Paper Quilt

"What makes me feel warm and snug is to think about pots full of honey," whispered Pooh in the darkness.

"What makes me feel warm and snug is to NOT think about not-warm and not-snug things," chimed in Piglet.

"What makes me feel warm and snug is to think about my friends," said Christopher Robin. And no one could argue with that.

Collect pictures of family and friends. Sew them together to create this festive paper Christmas quilt that can make Christmas last all year long. For extra fun, you can take it out next year and see how everyone has changed!

WHAT YOU NEED:

- A grown-up (very important!)
- Construction paper
- Ruler
- Safety scissors
- Hole punch
- Yarn or string
- Markers, crayons, pens, or pencils

WHAT YOU DO:

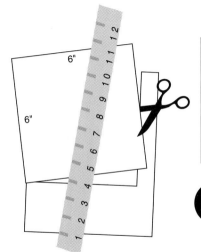

1 Measure and cut construction paper into 6 x 6-inch squares. A grown-up can help you measure.

2 Punch 5 holes on each edge.

3 Give each friend and family member a square and something to draw with. Ask each person to draw a picture of him– or herself on it. (That's called a self-portrait.) People can give you photographs of themselves if they prefer.

4 Thread yarn or string through the holes in the edges to sew the squares together into a quilt, as shown. It can be as large or small as you like. Make quilts for your stuffed animals or dolls, too!

81

Christopher Robin's Peanut-Butter Bird Feeder

"It's such a chilly day today," exclaimed Christopher Robin, rubbing his hands together to keep warm. "I'll bet the birds are hungry. All the seeds and berries they like to eat are frozen."

Here's a delicious bird feeder you can make to keep your feathered friends singing all winter!

WHAT YOU NEED:

- A grown-up (very important!)
- Ribbon
- Pinecone
- Peanut butter (smooth or chunky)
- Plastic knife
- Birdseed
- Paper plate

WHAT YOU DO:

1 Tie the ribbon around the top part of the pinecone so you can hang it.

2 Using the plastic knife, spread peanut butter over the whole pinecone.

3 Sprinkle birdseed onto the paper plate. Roll the sticky cone in the seeds until it's covered.

4 Hang your bird feeder outside, near a window, so you can watch all your new dinner guests.

83

We Wish You a Merry Christmas

We wish you a merry Christmas,

We wish you a merry Christmas,

We wish you a merry Christmas,

And a happy New Year!

We all know that Santa's coming,

We all know that Santa's coming,

We all know that Santa's coming,

And soon will be here.

The End

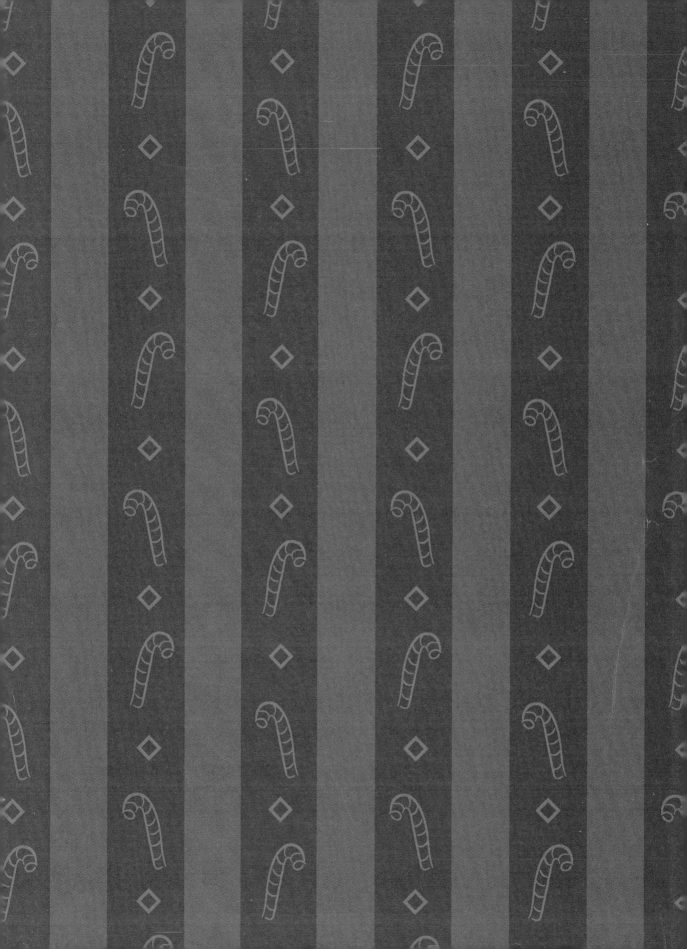